A Manual for Group Discussion Participants

Paul Bergevin
Professor of Adult Education
Indiana University

and

Dwight Morris
Assistant Professor of Adult Education
Indiana University

THE SEABURY PRESS   •   NEW YORK

Second Printing

510-567-Mu-3.5-3.5

Printed in the United States of America

Table of Contents

3

Part III. PHYSICAL ARRANGEMENTS

Part IV. APPENDICES

Introduction

Employing group discussion intelligently

This manual deals exclusively with group discusssion, and is for use where that technique is suited to the educational problem at hand.* Group discussion cannot be used indiscriminately to solve all adult educational problems. Group discussion, properly understood and conducted, is an effective technique for intelligent and productive self-expression. The informal relationships that result from the use of this technique are acceptable to adults and can help them to work toward effective personal and corporate action.

To be most effective, all participants should receive some training in the technique of group discussion. It is vital that *all* persons (called the participants) involved be trained, not just the leaders. Everyone receives the same kind of training; therefore, everyone is prepared to assume the various roles involved in group discussion if he so desires. In any case, every participant is acquainted with the responsibilities of everyone else. Part or all of this training may take place while the participants are engaged in the discussion program itself.

The participants in group discussion are sometimes called a learning team. This group of persons is composed of a leader, co-leader, observer, recorder, resource persons, and the group

---

* Bergevin and Morris, *Group Processes for Adult Education,* and Bergevin, Morris, and Smith, *Adult Education Procedures,* give criteria for deciding when this method can best be employed.

participants. These persons, if they are willing to study this technique, can help to train one another to become productive learners. Another way to receive the brief basic training necessary would be to secure the services of a person who is skilled in the use of this technique.

Without this training, leaders may dominate the meeting, or the group may break up into cliques; the resulting lack of cooperation will make it unlikely that the participants will make any progress, and dissension and misunderstanding may well result. Disappointment and frustration usually await groups which try to realize the benefits of this experience without the essential preparation.*

When group discussion has been chosen as the suitable educational technique, five points should be kept in mind as *minimum* essentials:

1. Have in mind a specific topic and goal
2. *Train* all participants; use two leaders, if possible
3. Select and use the best resource materials available
4. Evaluate the discussion meetings regularly
5. Do something with the results of the evaluation

Experiencing responsibility

We are told over and over that people will not accept responsibility. There is an element of truth in this statement. But what opportunity have they had to learn how to accept responsibility? As children, what responsibilities were they taught to accept in the home and

---

*Bergevin and McKinley, *Participation Training for Adult Education.*

6

in the school? As adults, what opportunities have they had to share responsibility on their jobs or in their churches? Too often they have been told *how* to do everything, with the result that they have lost much of the natural spirit of inquiry, which is one of the best allies of learning. Effective group discussion can help here.

If persons are given the opportunity, with intelligent guidance, to plan, organize, conduct, and evaluate their own programs of adult education, their programs are more likely to succeed than if dominated by "those who know." If they are to practice personal responsibility, they must come to know what responsibility is — not only by being told, but by experiencing it.

Telling and guiding

Many persons are too helpful in the wrong ways. It isn't an issue of helping people; it's how they are helped. It's a question of whether they are directed to wait for the oracle to speak, and, as a consequence, learn to depend on the oracle, or whether they are helped to develop a genuine love of inquiry and learning and encouraged to build their own educational structure. A case which illustrates this point: A person in charge of a certain organization was highly critical of a number of learning groups in the organization. When asked why, he said that he had given these groups "the answers" time and again; yet, listening to their discussion, he found that they did not seem to accept the answers he had given them.

7

A person does not necessarily understand and accept a fact or principle because he is told about it. A learner must come into a unique kind of relationship with the information to be learned. Sometimes telling or lecturing or sermonizing helps. Often, however, such techniques fail to stir a learner because these methods can be quite passive and impersonal.

Although group discussion plays only a limited role in the total learning process, it can, if properly conducted, call forth effort and responsibility from each learner. It has a tendency to personalize learning, a condition which is often lacking in more formal educational procedures. Certainly group discussion demands the attention of the learner. He can learn how to discipline himself and to help discipline others.

The discipline of effective group discussion can help to build confidence in the learner and to foster the desire to accept increasing responsibility.

Getting the "answers"

It is true that there are issues and questions at every group discussion session which cannot be settled, often because of the limited amount of time, and sometimes because the group lacks needed information. This apparent inefficiency naturally causes concern among persons unfamiliar with this learning procedure. Every educational approach has its limitations. No one procedure can provide the learner with all the answers every time he is exposed to the learning experience.

Skepticism concerning the use of group discussion for providing answers is closely allied with the problem of authoritarianism in teaching. Some people give lip service to group learning, but belie their position in the group by answering the questions without giving the others a chance to earn their conclusions. They may even go so far as to impose their views on members of the group. It is hard for one who is leading or observing a discussion group in action to restrain himself when he knows the answer — particularly when group members are struggling under self-imposed discipline to come to some understanding of the topic in their own way and according to their own abilities.

If a properly organized and conducted group seems unable to answer some of the questions which are posed, then it may be that, for the subject at hand, group discussion is not the educational technique to employ. All things, educationally speaking, cannot be accomplished with a discussion group any more than with a lecture or a panel type of meeting. Group discussion is a particular tool to be used for specific jobs.

However, when the group discussion technique is correctly applied, discussion meetings will often close with unanswered questions still disturbing the group. This is not necessarily bad. More often than not it has produced in the minds of the participants a desire to continue inquiry on their own initiative. Learning in this case does not stop when the discussion group breaks up.

Answers to particular problems are obtained, or further light is thrown on an issue, sometimes after the discussion group disbands, because some members continue to discuss the problem informally with each other. Between sessions, they seek information from resource materials — books, pamphlets, newspapers, magazines, etc. — and they consult privately with someone outside the group who may contribute information.

Two
leaders
are
effective

Effective discussion can be accomplished only when there is a degree of unity in the group. Active groups, however, often put a serious strain on harmony. Arranging for two leaders to work together can assist the group to maintain the degree of stability necessary to accomplish the desired results. Although the roles of each should not appear to be clear-cut, one leader can promote purposeful discussion and see that the objective is accomplished, and the other leader, as his main task, can "pour oil" on strained relationships.

Through experience with discussion groups, people can learn to arrive at their own answers. When members are given a chance (with moderate guidance) to work on their own, their efforts take on meaning, and they feel the satisfaction of accomplishment.

Goals
and
purposes

A goal is the ultimate objective. Every learning group must establish a goal at the start of the learning program. If a group fails in this regard, it will be unable to evaluate its progress at a later date. If a traveler didn't know where he was going, how would he know when he got there?

A group should determine where it wants to go, then at regular intervals take time out to evaluate — to determine how it is coming along toward accomplishing what it started out to do.

A purpose is a more limited or immediate task than a goal. What the group intends to do in order to arrive at the ultimate objective or goal may be called the purpose. Purposes are changed and adjusted as needed.

The basic idea to remember is that the group must establish some definite reason for its existence, and also some goal to be reached which will indicate the successful accomplishment of the stated reason. At regular intervals, a little time must be taken to determine the progress made (evaluation), and to make any adjustments and corrections necessary to keep on the course toward the goal.

PART I

The Group Discussion Technique

A. Definition of Group Discussion

Group discussion is purposeful conversation and deliberation about a topic of mutual interest among six to twenty trained participants under the guidance of a trained participant called a leader.

B. Purpose of Group Discussion

The purpose of group discussion is to provide a learning opportunity which emphasizes the relationship of the participants to one another through sharing and testing experiences.

C. Some General Characteristics of Good Group Discussion

1. Presupposes the selection of a topic by the group itself or by a planning committee
2. Presupposes some preparation on the subject by the leader and the group members
3. Establishes a natural, calm, and informal atmosphere conducive to learning
4. Includes questions and responses that come not from the leader but from the group
5. Encourages diversity of opinion
6. Emphasizes the importance of the individual
7. Involves thinking, reading, writing, listening, and speaking by all members of the group
8. Emphasizes learning rather than teaching
9. Brings the individual into a mature, working relationship with the group
10. Emphasizes the need to understand human relationships and to assume personal responsibility
11. Moves toward specific and purposeful goals determined by the group

D. Some Uses of Group Discussion

1. To develop a nucleus of individuals for leadership in an institution or community
2. To assist individuals to learn how to participate and how to express their opinions and ideas
3. To permit communication of ideas and information
4. To assist in the developing or modifying of attitudes of leaders toward participants and of participants toward leaders
5. To encourage and stimulate learning (in many subject areas) through direct participation
6. To teach skills for human relationships
7. To encourage and stimulate people to learn more about problems that concern their neighbors and fellow workers
8. To encourage and develop other informal discussion groups in neighborhoods, organizations, etc.
9. To identify a problem
10. To explore a problem
11. To solve a problem
12. To decide on a plan of action
13. To create or extend interest in a situation
14. To form the nucleus for a broad formal and informal program of adult education

E. Some Potential Results of Good Group Discussion

1. The purposeful exchange of ideas in an informal environment gives group members a better understanding of people.
2. The group finds areas of agreement through which effective action can be taken.
3. This educational process helps to avoid an embittered minority.
4. The group members learn to place a premium on trying to understand the other person and to appreciate his point of view rather than on dominating him or arguing with him.

5. The dignity of each person is enhanced through intelligent participation.
6. Good group discussion helps people develop exploratory and creative attitudes.
7. Group discussion assists adults to grow intellectually and emotionally by causing them to recognize a problem, face it, search for significant evidence, evaluate the evidence, and come to a mature conclusion.
8. Persons who have an opportunity to participate in good group discussion become less self-centered and more concerned about their fellow men. This results in learning to work together.
9. The recognition of the right to conform or dissent indicates growth in the knowledge of the democratic process.
10. Individuals learn to think for themselves and to assume personal responsibility.
11. Participants can acquire knowledge in the subjects discussed and in other related subjects.
12. When group discussion is properly conducted over a period of time, there is improvement in ability to see the types of problems which can be successfully handled.
13. Participants are better able to see life's fundamental relationships when they consider problems in a corporate situation; they are less prone to try to departmentalize knowledge.
14. Good group discussion tends to satisfy an individual's basic emotional need for security and self-esteem by bringing him to feel that he belongs to a group and that his opinions are valued by others.
15. In study-discussion groups involving several meetings, the participants accumulate a fund of knowledge through their discussions. This information should be recorded, reproduced, and distributed to the participants; thus, the contributions can become a permanent record for review by the original group and a resource for other persons or groups interested in the same subject area.

F. Advantages of Group Discussion

1. This technique provides those who use it with maximum opportunity for the acceptance of personal responsibility for learning.
2. A person can share his experience and opinions with others and get their reactions.
3. One can gain insight into his own behavior.
4. This technique encourages a person to develop his abilities to work as a member of a team.
5. This technique can assist a person to develop self-confidence in group situations.
6. Persons using this technique effectively usually establish friendship, understanding, and acceptance.

G. Limitations of Group Discussion

1. The technique is suitable only for groups of six to twenty persons.
2. Unproductive discussion often results when the participants have not had training in their roles and responsibilities.
3. The technique requires that all those taking part have or can acquire enough knowledge about the topic to permit meaningful discussion. Experience has revealed that often people will not take the time and care necessary to unearth facts in preparation for a group discussion session.
4. Some persons probably will not accept responsibility for the success of the discussion.
5. It is relatively easy for one or two persons to dominate the discussion.
6. This technique requires topics that lend themselves to discussion.
7. Like any procedure, it is unique and has specific uses. It is not a panacea for all educational problems.

PART II

The Participants in Group Discussion

A. The Leader and His Responsibilities

1. The leader is a trained participant who guides the discussion. He is not necessarily an expert in the subject or problem area from which the topic comes. He needs to have (or should be willing to acquire) enough knowledge to understand the significance of the topic and the issue that it suggests. It is important to remember that leadership is a role that a trained participant temporarily accepts. It is not a position that is permanently bestowed on someone. Most discussion groups rotate leadership in order to develop a broad base of competent leadership and provide as many persons as possible with insight into the problems and duties of the leader.

   Using two leaders. Often two persons guide a discussion, one termed the leader and the other the co-leader. The co-leader assists the leader in a way that seems appropriate in planning and conducting the discussion. He helps develop suggested purposes, an outline, and discussion questions. He may record the significant contributions made during the discussion on a blackboard or easel.

2. Some Qualities and Attitudes of a Good Leader*

   a. Should have a sincere interest in people

   b. Should have a sense of humor and use it

   c. Should be able to create a friendly atmosphere where people feel that they are welcome and that their contributions are valued

   d. Must indicate keen interest in the topic being discussed

   e. Should try to be lively and creative

   f. Must have a sense of purpose and direction

---

*See Appendix A.

16

g. Must be willing to master the technical aspects of leading group discussions

h. Must be able to make prompt decisions for guiding the group

i. Must be patient with the speed of the group

j. Should respect the opinions of others and try to be impartial

k. Should be a good listener

l. Should graciously accept ideas and comments with which he does not agree

m. Should resist any autocratic tendency that he finds in himself

n. Should try to draw out the opinion of the group

o. Should guard against trying to press his own ideas on the group

p. Should be willing to promote independent thinking within the group by encouraging an individual spirit of inquiry

q. Should realize that group discussion is not conducted to exalt the leader but to achieve the goals of its members

r. Should guard against talking too much, should stay in the background guiding the process, but focusing the attention on others and letting them take the credit

3. Major Reasons for Having a Trained Discussion Leader
A Leader Can:
a. Assist the group to arrive at consensus (if desirable and possible)

b. Stimulate purposeful talk

c. See to it that all persons participate freely

d. Act as a guide and helper

e. Handle "problem participants" intelligently

f. Assist the group to define and pursue a goal

g. Act as a catalyst in discussion

h. Establish and maintain good communication

i. Assist in alleviation of some tensions

4. Duties of the Leader
   a. The Leader Prepares for the Discussion
      (1) Gets information about the topic to be discussed
         (a) Becomes generally familiar with the topic
         (b) Gets information on all sides of the topic
         (c) Puts the principal ideas on paper
      (2) Makes careful plans for the discussion
         (a) Prepares a short outline as a guide, listing three or four main points
         (b) Prepares a few appropriate questions to start the discussion (based upon his outline)
         (c) Prepares introductory remarks
            . . *Brief* introduction of the topic to be discussed should include answers to the following questions:
            What is the purpose of this discussion?
            Why is the topic important?
               Length of introductory remarks will vary with interest, experience, and previous knowledge of group.
            . . Introduction sometimes built around appropriate visual aids (see Appendix E)
               . Supplementary visual materials must be directly related to the subject to be discussed.
               . Leader should prepare group for this kind of presentation so members will know how to use the materials as discussion aids.
               . Leader should ask pertinent questions about the visual aids used. These questions should be specific. They serve as a starting point for the main discussion.
         (d) Makes suitable physical arrangements
            . . Should see to it that chairs are arranged so that each group participant can see the

18

face of every other group participant without turning around (see illustrations on pages 29 and 30)

.. Should see that name cards are placed before each member of the group (see illustration on page 34)

(e) Plans for participation

.. Tries to get a group of optimum size (six to twenty persons)

.. Should recommend that members of the group, called group participants, prepare for the discussion by reading or in some way acquiring information about the topic

.. Should explain the group discussion technique; may explain briefly the duties and responsibilities of a group discussion leader and also what is expected of each group participant (see statement on the leader, page 36, also responsibilities of the group participant as outlined on page 24)

.. Should learn something of the interests, vocations, etc., of each participant present

b. The Leader Conducts the Discussion

(1) Before getting started

(a) Arrives in advance of meeting time and gets acquainted with the participants

(b) Makes sure that each participant introduces himself at the first meeting

(2) Starting the discussion

(a) Writes topic on blackboard and gives prepared introduction

(b) Presents outline of topic to group participants

(c) Asks stimulating or provocative questions

to draw the group participants into discussion (questions have been prepared in advance)

. . Directs each question to one of the group participants

. . Tries to phrase each in such a way that it cannot be answered simply by "yes" or "no"

(3) Maintaining a friendly and informal atmosphere

(a) The leader must be aware of the role he plays. He must keep in mind that how he acts and what he says will to a considerable extent determine the setting. At this point, there is a tendency for some leaders to act the part of the expert or to develop a teacher-student relationship. The leader, being aware of this danger, must be constantly on guard against assuming, or being forced into, a position harmful to good discussion.

(b) Group participants do not have to raise hands in order to be recognized, nor do they have to address the chair, stand, or observe any other formal procedure. In fact, such actions should be discouraged by the leader until they gradually disappear.

(c) The leader should listen attentively to what each participant has to say. If the leader shows interest in every comment, the group participants will see, *by example,* the importance of each contribution.

(d) If any person has difficulty in expressing a thought, the leader should assist him in a helpful and friendly manner to communicate.

(e) The leader uses appropriate humor occasionally.

(4) Helping to establish good communication

Each idea expressed should be clear to those who are listening. The leader:

20

(a) Sees to it that the group participants have an opportunity to get their pet ideas which are related to this topic "off their chests." This acts as a purgative and is sometimes necessary before the group will get down to the business at hand.

(b) Determines when to keep the discussion on the subject and when to allow digression. Occasional short digressions are natural and healthy in any discussion.

(c) Encourages and helps people to say what they mean. Restates comments (if necessary) to check for the intended meaning.

(d) Helps group participants to accept and evaluate criticism of their ideas. He discourages petty remarks which may arise from personality conflicts.

(e) Sets the pattern of communication by helping the group participants to share in the discussion — to share with all present.

(f) Uses simple, clear-cut language; doesn't try to show off his vocabulary.

(g) Does not evaluate or criticize comments offered by the group participants. He sees to it that the group participants do this job.

(5) Keeping the discussion moving

(a) The leader encourages *purposeful* talk throughout the discussion; mere talk is not good discussion.

(b) The leader maintains balanced participation

. . Anyone with something to contribute to the discussion should have an opportunity to say it.

. . The leader should speak and act as though he expects participation.

. . The leader should bring quiet or timid members into the discussion (see Appendix B).

21

. . The leader must see that every group participant sits with the group and remains a part of it (no fringe of non-participation or side discussion carried on in undertones).

. . The leader must keep discussion from becoming one-sided

. Encourages those who hold the minority position to participate, if encouragement is necessary; he can draw them into discussion by introducing ideas himself or by asking them what they think of the ideas which may have been presented.

. Guards against domination of the discussion by a small, articulate group, or by one person.

. Encourages the participants to assist all to contribute to the discussion and allow a reasonable time for each contribution.

(c) When the leader asks a question, he should pause momentarily, and if no one speaks, he can be silent until the pressure of silence makes someone talk, or he can direct a question to a particular person.

(d) The leader guides the discussion along the established outline

. . Should not hold too rigidly to the outline; on the other hand, should not allow too many digressions

. . Should encourage the group to decide whether the discussion is staying on the topic

. . Should see to it that the discussion flows along in a natural, not forced, manner

(e) The leader occasionally makes brief summaries (see page 31 on use of blackboard) which should be impartial and understandable by the group, in order to:

. . Help the group to stay on the topic

. . Prevent needless repetition

. . Assist in recording areas of agreement and disagreement

. . Prepare the group to pass from one part of the topic to another

(f) The leader remains in the background

. . Should talk only when necessary

. Makes no speeches after the brief introduction but gives brief comments, occasional summaries, and asks pertinent questions

. . Should provide direction and movement to the discussion through subtle suggestions. *He does not answer questions — he redirects them to other group participants.*

. . Should not assume the role of expert

(g) The leader constantly seeks from group participants information and evidence from which conclusions can be drawn.

(h) The leader concludes the meeting (it is suggested that each discussion period last no longer than one and one-half hours):

. . Should tie up loose ends of the discussion in a final summary; does not hand down his own conclusions but summarizes the contributions that came from the group

. . May point out the milestones that have been reached in considering the *subject* and point toward future *topics* which could derive from the same or *another subject*

23

. . Before the close of the meeting, the following questions must be talked over and agreed upon:

    . Why are we going to hold another meeting?

    . Where will the next meeting be held? At what time?

    . What will be the topic?

    . What resource materials should be read and where can the participants get these, or other kinds of needed information?

    . Should an expert (or experts) be called in at the next meeting as a resource person?

    . Who will be the leader at the next meeting?

B. The Group Participant and His Responsibilities

1. The group participants are those persons who take an active part in the discussion. They presumably are (a) interested in the topic, (b) willing to prepare for the discussion, and (c) willing to accept responsibility for sharing their ideas and opinions.

2. Responsibilities of the Group Participant

   a. The group participant should realize that he has a great deal to do with the success or failure of the discussion.

   b. The group participant must make an effort to become an active sharing member of the learning team.

   c. The group participant must come to the meeting prepared by having studied the appropriate resource materials.

   d. The group participant should be willing to learn to accept criticism of his ideas, and to comment on the ideas of others in an acceptable manner.

e. The group participant should discourage any attempts by the leader to teach (rather than to guide), or to distort the contributions of the group.

f. The group participant should be as specific as possible when making his contributions.

g. The group participant must recognize that discussion is not debate.

h. The group participant should use language which the group understands and speak in conversational tones.

i. The group participant is obligated to try to:
   . . Know himself better
   . . Know his fellow learners better
   . . Make his views known to others
   . . Respect the opinions of others
   . . Think for himself
   . . Cooperate in resolving problems

3. What the Group Participant May Expect

   a. To have a better understanding of himself and other people

   b. To acquire new learning skills and knowledge

   c. To learn how to work cooperatively with others in an attempt to solve problems of mutual interest

   d. To learn how to develop an idea and how to apply it to the point being discussed

   e. To discover applications that can be made to his personal problems

   f. To share responsibilities

   g. To be accepted by the group

   h. To be respected by the group

   i. To be disciplined when he deserves it

   j. To share his ideas and have them challenged

   k. To be permitted to substantiate his views when he agrees or disagrees with a point under discussion

   l. To learn how to arrive at consensus

C. The Recorder

1. The recorder is a participant who temporarily assumes the responsibility for recording such information as will assist the learning team in their discussion.

2. The Nature of the Recorder's Job
   a. The recorder does not participate in the discussion.
   b. The recorder's job is rotated at regular intervals. Ask for volunteers.
   c. The recorder should sit in a place where he does not distract the other participants.
   d. The recorder is not the secretary of the meeting and does not take verbatim notes.
   e. The recorder puts down points only when he is asked to do so by the participants.
   f. The recorder usually does not perform the same writing responsibilities as the leader or co-leader. The leader or co-leader records certain tentative contributions on the blackboard or easel. The recorder puts down points the group agrees to preserve or pursue further.

D. The Observer

1. The observer is a person who objectively watches others at work in this educational process for the purpose of improving communications and expediting problem solving.

2. The Nature of the Observer's Job
   a. Does not participate in the discussion
   b. Sits away from the group
   c. Keeps appropriate personal notes from which he explains his reactions
   d. Shares his reactions with the participants when asked to do so
   e. Watches the process only
   f. The observer looks for such things as:
      . . Reasonably balanced participation
      . . Domination by certain participants

26

.. Sharing responsibility by each group participant for the general success of the group

.. How the leader is doing his job (see Part II, Section A)

.. How well the group is prepared to discuss the subject

.. How side conversations, or speaking to one another in undertones, were controlled

.. How physical facilities were used

.. How well the group stayed on the subject

.. How well the group participants helped one another

.. How the group attacked issues which involved conflict and tension, and how these were handled by the leader

.. How withdrawal was treated by the leader and group participants

.. How the group accomplished what the group set out to do

E. The Resource Person

1. The resource person is an expert or authority who contributes information and opinion to participants in a learning situation.

When a topic cannot be treated fully by the group participants (because they lack knowledge or experience), it is well to invite a resource person to attend a meeting or two. He is most valuable to a discussion group when he makes knowledge available to the group on an informal basis and helps the group to clarify an issue through brief, well-chosen statements. He should remain in the background most of the time, ready to answer questions and provide information that would help them with their problem. He does not solve the problem for them. If it is necessary for the resource person to lecture to the group or to attend too many meetings, then group discussion is not the educational medium to be used. Some other procedure should be employed.

2. Characteristics of a Good Resource Person
    a. Should be a recognized authority or have more than average knowledge in the field being explored
    b. Should be willing and able to share his knowledge with the group
    c. Should be able to *listen* as well as to speak

3. When to Seek the Help of a Resource Person
    a. When the group has arrived at the point in their discussion where additional facts are needed and these facts are not available from usual sources (libraries, etc.)
    b. When the group seems to be drifting toward an unsound position because of improper use of facts at hand or lack of knowledge
    c. When the participants have certain questions on which they wish an informed opinion, a new point of view, an authoritative answer

4. When Not to Use a Resource Person
    a. When a lecture is indicated
    b. When the resource person is used as a substitute for required reading or research which should have been done by the group participants

PART III

Physical Arrangements

The physical arrangements for group discussion are important. The participants should be comfortably seated so that they face each other, if possible; *all* participants must be included (no fringe of nonparticipation).

A. How to Arrange Chairs, Tables, etc., for a Group Discussion

1. In the home
   Choose one or the other of the methods illustrated, if possible. If neither plan is possible, make the best of what you have, but always use a face-to-face seating arrangement.

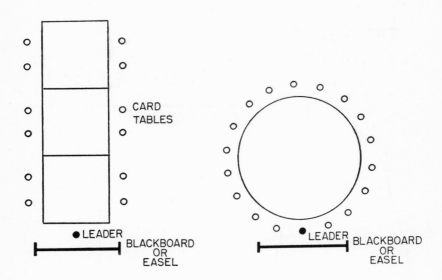

2. In the clubroom, hall, church, or school
   Choose one of the arrangements illustrated on page 30, if possible. In any case, keep in mind that a face-to-face arrangement is necessary.

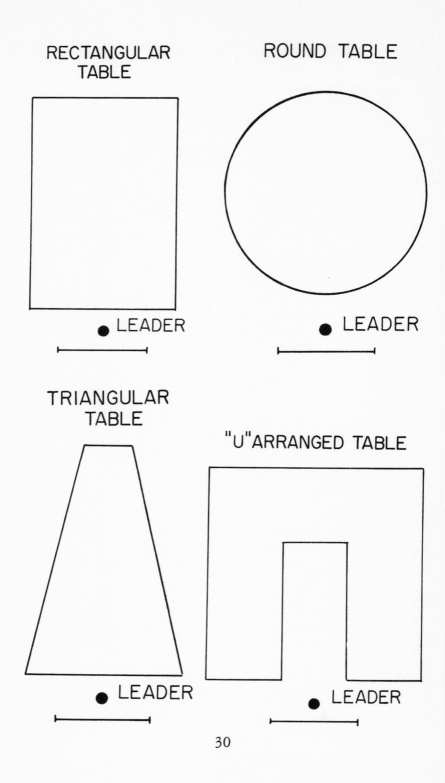

RECTANGULAR TABLE

ROUND TABLE

● LEADER

● LEADER

TRIANGULAR TABLE

"U"ARRANGED TABLE

● LEADER

● LEADER

30

B. How to Provide a Good Environment for Group Discussion

   1. Check list of items usually needed:
      Tables
      Chairs
      Blackboard or easel
      Chalk or crayon
      Eraser
      Ash trays
      Pencils
      Paper
      Name cards

   2. Other important factors:
      Adequate light
      Adequate heat and ventilation
      Shades or curtains (adjustable so sunlight does not cause discomfort)

C. How to Use the Blackboard or Easel for Group Discussion

The blackboard or easel is a tool of the leader, and he should use it to list all the contributions which will assist him and the group participants in evaluating the progress of the discussion and in summarizing the ideas presented. The leader may:

   1. Print or write his name (see illustration, page 32) at the top of the blackboard or easel

   2. Print or write the topic to be discussed

   3. Put a brief outline on the blackboard

   4. List the contributions of the group participants while each idea is in its formative stage:

      When further discussion of an idea is needed, he writes the idea on the blackboard and erases and corrects it until it accurately represents the ideas expressed by the group.

   5. Use the contributions listed on the blackboard or easel to:
      Make necessary summaries during the discussion to

evaluate the progress, to redirect the discussion, or to discipline the group participants.

Make a final summary at the conclusion of the meeting.

John Doe

Topic . . . .

Contributions

1. _____   5. _____

2. _____   6. _____

3. _____   7. _____

4. _____   8. _____

PORTABLE
BLACKBOARD

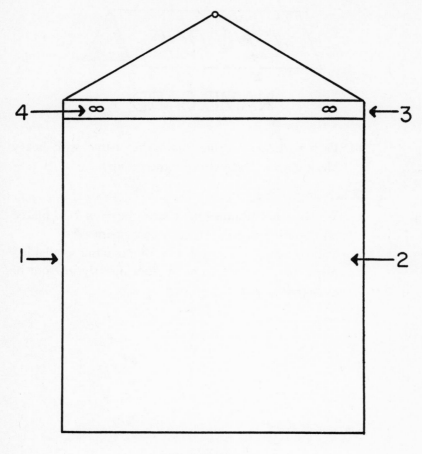

EASEL

1. Plywood back
2. Several sheets of wrapping paper
3. Wood slat
4. Two bolts and wing nuts

D. The Name Card

The name card is a device used to assist the participants in readily calling one another by name. It is courteous to a person to use his name.

1. How the name card is made:

   a. Provide each participant with a 3 x 5 card, which he folds lengthwise (see illustration, page 34)

NAME CARD

    b. Each participant prints his or her name with heavy black crayon (provided for the group)

2. Where to put the name card:
    a. When seated around a table have the name card placed on the table in front of each participant
    b. When seated in a circle (with no table available) place the name cards on the floor directly in front of each participant

PART IV

Appendices

A. The Leader in Group Discussion

B. Problem Participants

C. The Selection and Use of a Topic

D. Resource Materials

E. How to Use Audio-Visual Materials

F. A Sample Leader-Planned Discussion

G. Evaluating Group Discussion

H. Suggested Readings

I. A Glossary of Terms Relating
to Group Discussion

The Leader in Group Discussion

Some persons have the personality traits and the past training that fit them to act as leaders. They recognize that true leadership means assisting others to express themselves, guiding them intelligently, and pointing the way toward cooperative, harmonious action within the group. The spirit and nature of their leadership are in harmony with values essential to cooperative living.

Against this picture of leadership, we have the so-called leaders who are more concerned with personal advantage than with the benefits they can render to others. Visions of grandeur have ruined the effectiveness of many leaders. Others understand leadership to mean only domination. Persons who have little faith in humanity are likely to believe in, and to practice, a form of leadership which fails to let others develop to their full stature. Such lack of regard for others usually results in a retarded organization or in a community dependent on these leaders. Leaders who seem to have all the answers and who spoon-feed their followers may eventually impair the personal dignity of the group participants, and cause their disintegration into followers and nothing more.

There are dangers in extremes. In one instance, the leader might interpret his task as one which calls for the exercising of strong disciplinary techniques and the use of arbitrary methods. At the other end of the scale, we find leaders who are so anxious to be democratic that they provide little or no real leadership. These latter persons accept the responsibility of leadership but fail the persons they should serve by letting the groups become so disorganized that they become anarchical. To believe that anyone can say anything on any subject at any time he pleases before any group he selects is to confuse liberty with license. Such a view fails to keep privilege aligned with responsibility. The leader who recognizes the need for a limited amount of discipline along with organization and purposeful free expression senses the essence of leadership. Under good leadership, discipline is often self-imposed.

When a group is just beginning, real leadership, as we usually think of the term, is definitely needed. As the group progresses, a good leader begins to drop his role as leader and to establish himself in the role of guide and helper. He watches for clues that the group is maturing in the co-operative experience and gradually turns over a great part of the responsibility to the group, where it should reside. When this point is reached the title "leader" is perhaps a misnomer, for the so-called leader is more a helper and guide than he is a leader, according to the definition we usually associate with this word.

In many instances, persons hesitate to serve as leaders because they say they are not good talkers. Sometimes this apparent limitation is a striking advantage. *Most leaders talk entirely too much.* There are also many other reasons given by timid persons for escaping their responsibility to assume leadership. Although it is true that some persons can do a better job at leadership than others, it is nevertheless equally true that a great number of citizens who are not actively engaged in corporate activities could do an acceptable job of leadership if they had some training and were willing to try.

A participant who takes the role of a leader should consider himself as a helper, or one who assists other persons to develop and grow. When he violates this position and attempts to control the group for his personal ends, he is no longer useful in the leadership role.

It is highly recommended that all participants — the leader, the group participant, the observer, the recorder, and the resource person — receive some instruction in participation training. Participation training covers all the roles of the learning group — not just leadership. All participants, therefore, are acquainted with the leader's role as well as with the other roles.

There are three advantages to this idea of participation training:

1. The leader plays his role properly. He cannot run away with the group. The group participants see to this because they also have been trained in leadership.

2. More help is given to the leader by the group participants because they recognize their responsibilities better. They don't just sit and wait for the leader to teach them.

3. More leaders are available since all the participants have had training in the total process, not just leadership alone, but in all facets of this cooperative way of learning. They have been taught to take an active role as group participants, to act as observer or recorder, and to lead the group if they wish to or if called upon to do so.

Problem Participants Commonly Encountered and Suggestions for Dealing with Them

When helping the participants to become adjusted to learning together, don't try to push too hard. Remember that people are as they are, not as you might like them to be. Understanding and patience are important traits for a discussion leader to cultivate. He must learn to expect differences in the personality traits of group members. Uniqueness (within limits) is a precious asset to human personality. It must be preserved if group discussion is to fulfill its true function.

1. **The quiet person**

   This person is often timid and sometimes inarticulate. The expression of ideas while in the company of others may be difficult for him. Lead this person into the discussion by starting a friendly conversation with him before the session, if possible. During the discussion, direct toward him questions that cannot be answered by "yes" or "no," but require a statement of fact or opinion. Use a friendly tone of voice and be sincere. Build up confidence in this person by helping him defend and clarify his statements; then gradually guide him to the point where he will be on his own.

2. **The talkative person and the attention seeker**

   These types of persons often talk too much or talk for the purpose of drawing attention to themselves. Ideas that are presented will be reiterated and expanded on, or extended to a point where there is a complete departure from the subject being discussed. Ask others if they think the talker's ideas are pertinent or relevant and in what way. Often these persons are nervous and talk to relieve their tensions. Allow them to do a reasonable amount of talking; then ask for another's ideas, and another's, until you think their participation is again advisable.

3. **The troublemaker**
This person is one who lacks certain social graces. He is often a table-pounder, sometimes as user of obscene or off-color language, often a "frank" talker who has little regard for the feelings of others. Usually, this person is easily identified by his fellow learners. Ordinarily, they are able to keep him under control by interrupting him or going on to a different point in the discussion. Sometimes it may be necessary for the leader to speak to him privately.

4. **The emotional person**
This person sometimes has trouble expressing his thoughts and becomes excited; the harder he tries, the less successful he is. He reveals his tension by blushing or talking fast or loudly or incoherently. Don't joke about this person's mistakes or shortcomings. Come to his rescue in critical situations until he is able to express himself confidently in the group.

5. **The theoretical person**
This person expounds his own theories, or recites others which often have little or no bearing on the problem or its solution. The leader and the group participants should ask him for the evidence for his statements and to explain more concisely what he means, or how they apply in the situation under discussion.

6. **The formalist**
This person has experienced only formal educational programs where someone lectured or where it was necessary to abide by highly formalized rules of procedure. He may try to get the leader to answer all questions. Assist him to become acquainted with group discussion. From time to time, some persons may have to be instructed in the technique of group discussion.

7. **The minuteman**

   This person renders snap judgments about many ideas that are presented. Thoughtful consideration is too slow for him. But you will find that this type of person often has a good sense of humor. It is through this that the leader and group participants can help him to become a contributing member of the group.

8. **The fence-straddler**

   This person is characterized by unwillingness or inability to stand on his own beliefs and to express an opinion without qualifications. He is afraid of having others in the group disagree with him. This characteristic is very much in evidence when the "boss" is in the group or when some person of prominence is present. This person needs help, and assistance should come from the person who is causing the difficulty. The leader should ask the person who might be responsible for this situation to help by encouraging the fence-straddler to join in without fear of reprisals. Some straddlers are not necessarily afraid of anyone; they just can't make up their minds. Participation sometimes helps them because it gives them a chance to see and hear others expressing opinions and giving evidence of having some courage.

9. **The buffoon**

   This person is often jovial and good-natured, and he relishes the opportunity to make a pun or tell a joke. Although appropriate humor plays an important role in a discussion, too much is an interference. Such persons can usually be handled by the other group participants. If the group participants feel that the subject being discussed demands their serious attention, all "funny business" will usually come to an end. It helps for the leader to ask questions in a calm and serious tone.

10. **The superior person**

    Because of his educational background, his social or economic standing in the community, or his personal feeling of importance (which may be a figment of his imagination), this person has difficulty in adjusting to a democratic technique like group discussion. He feels superior to the participants, the topic, and the technique being used. He frequently does not work well with people. Find an area which is allied to that being studied and in which he has an interest, and ask him to contribute from his background of information and experience. This will probably satisfy his need to feel important. At the same time, it will involve him in the discussion in a worth-while way. As he works with the group participants, he may become less self-centered and assume a more productive role.

11. **The negative person**

This person thinks and talks in a negative manner, prefixing his statements with "don't do this," or "we can't do that," or, "we tried that and it won't work." He can create group pessimism, or a growing resentment which may cause a complete breakdown of the group. He will usually agree with any person who takes a negative stand. He sometimes styles himself as the devil's advocate. He is probably disturbed. This person can be helped by restating (or by asking him to restate) his contributions in a positive way and by assuring him of the worth of his new comments.

12. **The domineering person**

This person is sometimes in a position of authority in his everyday life and consciously or unconsciously carries over certain characteristics to the discussion meeting. He will often try to dominate the discussion as well as other members of the learning team. This person probably has executive ability and the ability to organize his thoughts; he should be able to contribute much to the discussion if he is handled properly. The leader may have to talk with him, reminding him of the purposes of group discussion. Show him that, although his ideas may be valuable, his way of presenting them could stand improvement.

13. **The politician**

This person is likely to attach himself to persons, ideas, or causes which seem to be most beneficial or expedient to him.

He is not troubled with fine-line distinctions between principles. This person is often a skilled rationalizer. He can make his position sound good. He has to be taught how to work with others in an open and honest atmosphere, this helping him to see the value of interests beyond his own.

14. **The overzealous optimist**

    An extremist in any direction can be harmful to a learning group. The person who sees everything as wonderful lacks objectivity as does the one who sees everything as bad. Escape from reality can be partially controlled by the group participants and the leader's helping these people to examine proposals carefully and critically. Emphasis can be placed on a reasonable amount of objectivity. This kind of emphasis needs to be repeated constantly.

No one of the characteristics described above will appear singly in a person. People tend to exhibit a combination of them. This brief survey of problem participants is not comprehensive, but represents a few general observations. The leader should guard against trying to classify persons in neat compartments, and, further, he should not concern himself with the therapist's role.

A leader will often need tact and ingenuity in dealing with serious problem participants, who, fortunately, are a minority in any group.

APPENDIX C

The Selection and Use of a Topic for Group Discussion

A topic should be selected which lends itself to group discussion. Usually, it would not be appropriate, for example, to use a topic like "Recent Changes in the Foreign Policy of Iran" for group discussion. We don't know enough about this subject area. A speech by an expert followed by a forum period would probably be best in this case. However, such a topic as "What Can We Do to Better Understand Our Foreign Neighbors?" might be pursued by group discussion. Even a long-term program consisting of many meetings and topics can be a profitable educational experience through group discussion if the topics selected are appropriate to the technique used.

1. **The topic should be selected carefully.**
   . . It should be appropriate to group discussion.
   . . It should be appropriate to the persons concerned (their background, interests, etc.).
   . . It should be selected or approved by those who are to participate in the discussion.
   . . It should be a topic which can be discussed. ("Why 2 + 2 = 4" would not arouse much enthusiasm, but "How Can We Organize and Start an Effective Adult Education Program in Our Church?" would command the attention of a number of groups interested in church activities.)
   . . It should have specific meaning and value to the group, institution, or community.
   . . It should be relatively concise, simply and clearly worded.

.. The topic should be one for which appropriate educational materials are available to enrich the discussion (i.e., books, pamphlets, films, phonograph records, magazine and newspaper articles, slides, etc.).

2. **The topic should be limited.**

   .. If the subject area suggested is too broad, it can be subdivided and one phase taken up at a time.

   .. If the subject requires a series of discussion sessions, the topic for each should be as self-contained as possible, yet an integral part of the over-all series.

   .. Generally, it is well to select a topic which can be discussed in a limited period of time (for example, one and one-half hours).

3. **How to use the topic.**

   .. The first and preliminary step is to explore the resource materials which will help enliven the topic (see Appendix D).

   .. Then provide group members with resource materials whenever possible.

   .. When desirable, ask a participant to study some definite aspect of the topic and present his findings.

   .. The discussion leader presents a brief introduction to the subject when the group convenes.

   .. The topic should be the focal point of the discussion. If the group strays too far from the topic, the discussion is usually fruitless.

   .. In the short evaluation period usually held at the end of each discussion session, progress made in pursuing the goal is taken into consideration.

Resource Materials

Resource materials are essential to group discussion.

Resource materials include books, pamphlets, films, slides, magazine and newspaper articles, posters, charts, graphs, exhibits, selected radio and television programs, recordings, etc. One or more of these learning aids is used in nearly all carefully planned and conducted group discussions. The way resource materials are selected and used for group discussion often means the difference between a profitable educational experience and a "gab fest."

People cannot talk intelligently about, or help each other to learn, something which they do not themselves know. Even if the participants are fairly well informed in a certain subject area, there are usually up-to-date resources which, if examined, will broaden their view and increase their worth as participants. It is the discussion leader's responsibility to see to it that someone secures and distributes resource materials to the group, or to indicate clearly where such materials can be obtained. And, further, the leader should constantly encourage the group to use these materials. Make use of the help which the local public library provides.

Sometimes the leader selects the resource material, and sometimes the leader and the group make the selection together. It depends on the nature of the subject, the accessibility of material, the character of the group, etc.

Some general suggestions follow:

1. **Printed material**

    . . Consult the local or state library or a specialized source (depending on the topic to be used) for suggestions of available printed materials on the subject.

.. If available in quantity and cheaply, printed material may be secured in advance and distributed to the group by the leader. Or copies of selected materials may be duplicated for distribution. Or the leader may indicate at an early session where material can be obtained and place the responsibility for securing it on each participant. Suggestions of pertinent materials should be solicited from the participants. Each participant should have a copy of the material when possible, preferably a copy that he can mark up if it is to be studied in detail.

.. The leader or a group participant informs the group about the purpose and use of the particular materials.

.. The leader encourages the participants to recognize the necessity of reading the selected materials, reminding them that each of them has a specific responsibility to himself and his group to make adequate preparation.

2. **Films, film strips, slides (see Appendix E)**

3. **Posters, charts, graphs**

.. On hundreds of subjects of community interest, posters, charts, or graphs are obtainable from associations of various kinds, from large business organizations, and from the state library. Consult the librarian and local affiliates of organizations or businesses for possibilities. Or the leader may arrange to have such visual materials made up by high-school art classes or by volunteers.

.. The leader should obtain visual aids that relate specifically to the topic.

.. These resource materials should be displayed in a conspicuous place while they are being used, but removed from view immediately after their use. If allowed to remain, they are a distracting influence.

47

How to Use Audio-Visual Materials

How to Use a Film for Group Discussion:

Using a film to encourage and stimulate group discussion is sometimes desirable. Films are useful when they directly concern the subject to be discussed; and even films that are not closely allied to the subject sometimes can be adapted to the discussion. In choosing a film, the leader should of course be careful to avoid having just another picture show.

When using a film to set the stage for a group discussion, the leader or a committee from the group should:

1. Carefully select the film

2. Preview the film (more than once if necessary)

3. Prepare a few questions for starting and maintaining the discussion

4. Write the questions on a blackboard or easel (before the meeting)

5. Introduce the subject and prepare the group to view the film by telling them what to look for

6. Show the film
   This should be done at the beginning of the meeting. Some precautionary steps to observe:
   a. Have the projector threaded and tested before the group arrives.
   b. Check the source of electricity.
   . . Is the correct voltage available?
   . . Will the outlet furnish current when the lights are out?
   . . Will there be enough light for the participants to take notes (if necessary)?
   . . Can the room be adequately ventilated during the showing?

7. The leader should not attempt to start the discussion as soon as the film is over and the lights are turned on. This sudden change from darkness and fixed attention calls for guidance; it is wise to allow a few minutes for the reorientation of the group.

8. Start the discussion
   a. During this orientation period, the leader should introduce the subject and give reasons for having used the film.
   b. Bring into view the questions on the blackboard or easel. Read these with the group and ask for additional questions to be added to the others.
   c. Lead the discussion as in any other situation.

9. Evaluate
   a. The film (see page 60)
   b. The discussion (see page 52)

The Use of Recording Equipment:

It is sometimes desirable to use a tape recorder to:

. . Present authoritative information available from reference sources in this form. Recordings give participants access to information in a group situation which the reading of printed materials cannot duplicate.

. . Study information brought to the group by a resource person.

. . Record and play back a group discussion for evaluative purposes.

. . Provide a permanent record of the proceedings.

Recording the proceedings of a discussion may be disadvantageous because:

. . This device may be a barrier to participation.

After the sessions have been held for some time and the group participants have found themselves, recording of proceedings may continue without disturbing the discussion flow.

A Sample Leader-Planned Discussion

Leader: John Doe.

Length of Discussion: 1½ hours.

Time: 7:30 P.M.

Date: November 15, 1965.

Place: The home of Mr. H. G. Jones, 2517 South Main Street.

Topic: Do we need a new sewer in our section of town? If so, what can we do about it?

1. **Introduction (by the leader, usually)**

   Some twenty-five years ago, our city constructed a sewer in this part of town to serve, at that time, seventy-five families. Now there are 350 families using this service. Especially during flash floods, we notice the inadequacies of our present system.

   The city engineer advises me that an adequate new sewer will cost approximately $100,000 or about $300 a family.

   With these facts in mind and in the light of our personal experiences, let us first discuss the need for a new sewer, and then proceed to set up certain goals toward which we can all work if action is agreed upon.

2. **Questions to start the discussion**

   . . Why do we need a new sewer?

   . . Can we as individuals afford a new sewer?

   . . How can this project be financed so the people in lower income brackets can afford to participate?

   . . How can we initiate action?

   These questions were prepared before the meeting and placed on the blackboard, or different individuals may have been asked in advance to think about and present each question.

3. **Discussion**

   The leader encourages first one and then another to speak on each of the questions presented at the beginning or raised in the group, endeavoring always to keep the group progressing toward a solution, *their* solution, or at least toward a realization of the sewage problem and the need for further consideration of it.

4. **Summary**

   Summarize the contributions of the group, noting them on the blackboard.

5. **Conclusion**

   The meeting should be concluded at a reasonable hour and at a point when enthusiasm is high. When concluding the meeting, establish:

   . . Whether or not another meeting is necessary for the completion of the discussion and planning.

   . . When will it be held (date and time)?

   . . Where will it be held?

   . . Who will act as leader?

   . . Topic?

   . . Resource persons or materials needed?

Evaluating Group Discussion

1. **What is evaluation?**

   Evaluation is the process of carefully appraising a situation by ascertaining the values accruing from it. In other words, how well did we accomplish what we set out to do? How close have we come to our goals?

2. **Why should we evaluate?**

   Any worth-while educational program should be evaluated to show the direction it is taking, to look for desirable new or different approaches, to show the impact of the program to date, and to indicate progress and determine needs.

3. **What do we evaluate?**

   We should evaluate in our educational programs their direction and meaning; the effectiveness of all the participants: the group participants, the leader, the observer, the recorder, the resource person, and the procedures used; the learning that has taken place; and whether or not we are successfully moving toward the goal we established.

4. **What method of evaluation should be used?**

   The method of evaluation should be determined by a careful study of the goals of the program. When choosing an evaluation device, consider the following factors: the size of the group to be measured, the purpose of the evaluation, the goals of the program, and the action which has resulted in pursuit of the goals.

   Some of the methods of evaluation that can be easily administered are: the check list, the questionnaire, the numerical chart, and the personal interview.

5. **Who evaluates?**

   A person or persons selected by the group should be made responsible for the evaluation. Care should be exercised to see to it that evaluation is not done by administrators exclusively.

6. **When to evaluate?**

Discussion programs cannot be adequately measured until the group has met several times and at least some of the participants have acquired new skills, attitudes, or information.

Time should be frequently set aside for the participants to re-examine their goals and to determine if they are on the right road to accomplishing the job they set out to do.

7. **How to evaluate?**

See points enumerated in 3 above.

Sample evaluation devices are illustrated on the following pages.

HOW TO EVALUATE
(A Questionnaire)
Evaluation Sheet for Group Discussion Leaders

I. Introduction   Yes No

   A. Was the topic chosen appropriate to the group? .... ____ ____

   B. Was the topic presented well (briefly and specifically)? .... ____ ____

   C. Was the purpose of the discussion explained? .... ____ ____

II. Participation

   A. Did every member contribute to the discussion? .... ____ ____

   B. Were various sides of the question brought out? .... ____ ____

   C. Did the leader impose his views? .... ____ ____

   D. Did the participants present their contributions reasonably, with supporting data? ... ____ ____

   E. Was anyone permitted to dominate the discussion? .... ____ ____

   F. Did the leader let the discussion get off the track? .... ____ ____

   G. Did the leader present occasional summaries to help guide the group? .... ____ ____

   H. Did the leader make a speech? .... ____ ____

III. Summary

   A. Did the leader present a short final summary? .... ____ ____

   B. Did the summary represent group views? ____ ____

IV. Purpose

   A. Did the group:

      1. Work along the line presented by the leader? .... ____ ____

      2. Demonstrate an interest in it? ...... ____ ____

      3. Identify the problem? .... ____ ____

4. Explore the problem? .... ____ ____
5. Analyze the problem? .... ____ ____
6. Attempt the solution of the problem? ____ ____
7. Extend their present interest in the problem or situation? .... ____ ____
8. Assemble information only? ...... ____ ____
9. Work as a unit? .... ____ ____
10. Act as a decision-making body? ..... ____ ____
11. Determine a course of action? ...... ____ ____

B. Did the discussion point toward further discussion? .... ____ ____

V. Other Important Factors
A. Did the leader use the blackboard? ...... ____ ____
B. Did the meeting start and stop on time? ... ____ ____
C. Were the physical arrangements adequate (room temperature, light, blackboard, table)? .... ____ ____
D. Was the resource person forced into the role of speechmaker? .... ____ ____
E. Did the group:
1. Plan the next meeting? .... ____ ____
2. Arrange for the next leader? ...... ____ ____
3. Decide on materials to be used? .... ____ ____
4. Select a date for the next meeting? ... ____ ____

HOW TO EVALUATE
(A Numerical Chart)

1. How did you like today's discussion? It was

6	5	4	3	2	1	0
excellent	fine	good	fair	not so good	poor	very poor

2. Did you gain any new ideas or concepts from the discussion?

6	5	4	3	2	1	0
many	several	quite a few	some	not many	few	none

3. Did the discussion help clarify any problems? It was

0	1	2	3	4	5	6
useless		not too helpful		of some help		very helpful

4. Were you interested in the discussion topic?

6	5	4	3	2	1	0
very much		quite a bit		not much		not at all

5. How well do you think the participants worked together?

6	5	4	3	2	1	0
very well		fairly well		average		poorly

6. How would you rate the discussion leader?

0	1	2	3	4	5	6
very poor	poor		fair		good	excellent

Please do not sign your name. If you have any further suggestions, write them here.

HOW TO EVALUATE

Chart for Registering the Participation of Each Individual and
Evaluating the Degree of Balance in the Discussion

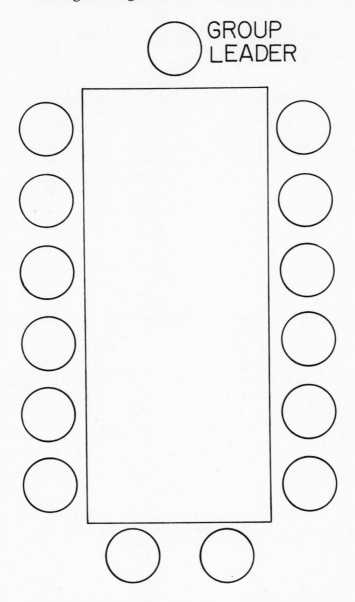

(See next page for the chart of an actual meeting)

HOW TO EVALUATE

Completed Chart for Evaluating Individual Participation and Balance in a Discussion

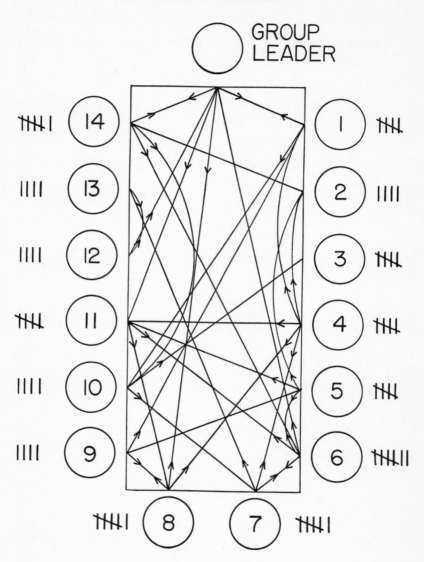

HOW TO EVALUATE

Questionnaire to be Used to Evaluate a Completed Series of Study-Discussion Meetings

Please take about fifteen minutes to complete this questionnaire.

1. Do you feel that this series of meetings contributed something to you by:

   Giving you more information? Yes_____ No_____
   Changing your ideas? Yes_____ No_____
   Changing your attitudes? Yes_____ No_____
   Adding skills (discussion)? Yes_____ No_____

2. What are your personal views concerning the value of the series? (check one)
   a. Decidedly advantageous
   b. Advantageous
   c. Worth-while
   d. Of no value

3. What is the most important value, or values, you received from this series?

4. What suggestions can you give for a future discussion series?
   a. Discussion topics:
   b. What films?
   c. Other media which you would like to see employed:
      Speech . . . .
      Panel . . . .
      Symposium . . . .
      Colloquy . . . .
      Forum . . . .
      Others . . . .

5. If your answers to question 1 and/or 2 are negative — what suggestions do you have for improving the process?

6. Other comments.

Please do not sign your name.

HOW TO EVALUATE
(A Numerical Chart)

How to Evaluate a Film as an Aid Toward Motivating Participation

1. How did you like the film?

6	5	4	3	2	1	0
excellent	fine	good	fair	not so good	poor	very poor

2. Did you feel that the film was appropriate?

6	5	4	3	2	1	0
yes		somewhat			no	

3. Do you think the film was helpful to the discussion?

0	1	2	3	4	5	6
useless	not too helpful		of some help		very helpful	

4. Do you feel that proper use was made of the film by the leader?

6	5	4	3	2	1	0
excellent use		some use		improper use		no use

Please do not sign your name. If you have further suggestions to make, write them here.

List of Suggested Readings

Bergevin, Paul, and McKinley, John. *Design for Adult Education in the Church.* Seabury Press, New York, 1961, 320 pp.

Bergevin, Paul, and McKinley, John. *Participation Training for Adult Education.* Bethany Press, St. Louis, Mo., 1965.

Bergevin, Paul, and Morris, Dwight. *Group Processes for Adult Education.* Seabury Press, New York, 1960, 86 pp.

Bergevin, Paul; Morris, Dwight; and Smith, Robert M. *Adult Education Procedures.* Seabury Press, New York, 1963, 245 pp.

Bonner, Hubert. *Group Dynamics.* Ronald Press, New York, 1959, 531 pp.

Lasker, Bruno. *Democracy Through Discussion.* H. W. Wilson Company, New York, 1949, 376 pp.

Leadership Pamphlets, Adult Education Association of the U.S.A., Washington, D.C.

Liveright, A. A. *Strategies of Leadership,* Harper & Row, New York, 1959, 135 pp.

Ross, Murray G., and Hendry, Charles. *New Understandings of Leadership.* Association Press, New York, 1957, 158 pp.

Thelen, Herbert A. *Dynamics of Groups at Work.* University of Chicago Press, Chicago, 1954, 370 pp.

A Glossary of Terms Relating to Group Discussion

Adult Education: The process through which adults have and use opportunities to learn systematically under the guidance of an agency, teacher, or leader; experiences in day-to-day living which cause adult behavioral change; the study of the professional field of adult education; in a free society a kind of education which promotes a mature rationality in our adult lives and institutions.

Aids, Educational: Resources such as pamphlets, exhibits, annotated bibliographies, case histories, audio-visual materials, and information briefs, which assist in the learning process through the employment of the several senses.

Authority: An accepted source of information, direction, or guidance.

Co-Leader: In group discussion, if two persons share leadership, they are called co-leaders. Sometimes one is called a leader and his helper is called co-leader.

Communication: A process by which people influence one another by transmitting and receiving ideas, opinions, feelings, and attitudes.

Communication, Pattern of: A systematic arrangement which defines the origin, direction, and end of the flow of verbal participation by the members of a learning group.

Consensus: A working agreement or concord, often of a tentative nature but sufficiently valid to accommodate persons of different viewpoints.

Content: Mainly the substantive information (subject matter) in a learning program; the "what" of education as compared with the "how." The "what" may be considered content; the "how," process. In program planning, content means the topics developed for treatment in the learning activity being planned.

Evaluation: Judging the effectiveness of an adult education experience in terms of the goals.

Goal: The objective or end toward which a learning experience is directed, the expected results; a specific statement of intention to meet a need.

Group Discussion: A purposeful conversation and deliberation about a topic of mutual interest among 6 to 20 trained participants under the guidance of a trained participant called a leader.

Group Participant: A member of a learning team who takes an active part in the educational process as one of the learners in the group.

Issue: A presentation of alternatives between which the persons in a group may choose or decide.

Leader: Any member of a learning team who accepts the responsibilities of leading the other participants in adult educational endeavors.

Observer: A trained person in an educational program who objectively watches and listens to the forces at work in a learning group.

Participant: A person trained as a member of a learning team. All the members of the learning group are participants assuming different roles: group participants, leaders, resource persons, and observers.

Participation: The sharing of a variety of responsibilities in an educational venture.

Procedure: A systematic series of steps designed to accomplish a task.

Process: The procedural intrapersonal and interpersonal factors involved in how a person learns in contrast to what he learns (content).

Purpose: The immediate task that will be performed in an educational program; differs slightly from "goal" and "objective" in that these terms often refer to ultimate outcome. Purpose is sometimes called declaration of intent.

63

Recorder: A participant who accepts the responsibility to write down the salient points that emerge during the course of an adult learning experience. The participants can make use of this information for summarizing and keeping a permanent record.

Resource: Educational material or aid from which persons in an educational situation may seek information. The adult educator uses such resources as audio-visual materials, printed matter, charts, graphs, and maps.

Resource Person: An expert or authority who contributes information and opinion to participants.

Technique: The way in which the adult educator arranges the relationships of learners and resources to assist the learners to acquire knowledge in a learning situation.

Topic: In group discussion the main subject, problem, or issue to be discussed. In program planning, defines the desired information — the problems, issues, questions, and concepts — which the program will treat (i.e., the topics represent the potential content of the program).